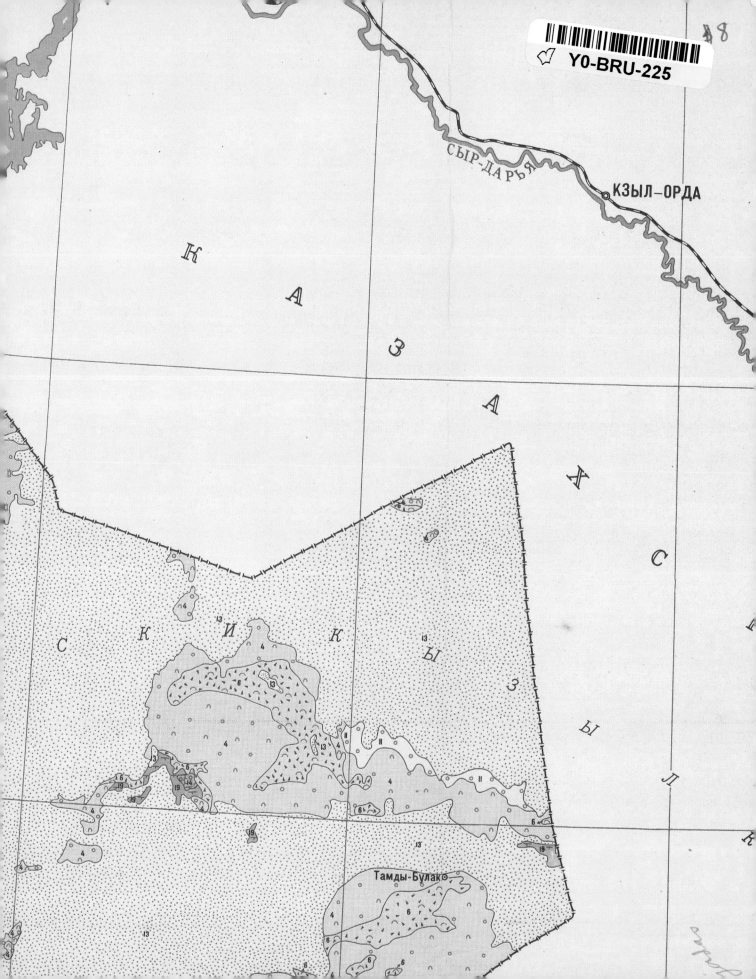

СЫР-ДАРЬЯ

КЗЫЛ—ОРДА

К

А

З

А

Х

С

С

К

И

К

Ы

З

Ы

Л

Тамды-Булак

ALL THE COLORS OF THE RAINBOW.

UZBEKISTAN IKATS FROM THE COLLECTION OF PEGGY SLAPPEY

EDITED BY
DONALD A. WOOD, PH.D

CONTRIBUTIONS BY
ALI ISTALIFI, PEGGY SLAPPEY, AND DON WOOD

 BIRMINGHAM MUSEUM OF ART · BIRMINGHAM · ALABAMA

ALL THE COLORS
OF THE RAINBOW

This catalogue has been published in conjunction with the exhibition *All the Colors of the Rainbow: Uzbekistan Ikats from the collection of Peggy Slappey* organized by the Birmingham Museum of Art, Birmingham, Alabama, March 19–July 10, 2016.

© 2016 Birmingham Museum of Art
www.artsbma.org

First published in 2016
by the Birmingham Museum of Art
2000 Rev. Abraham Woods Jr. Blvd
Birmingham, AL 35203

ISBN-13: 978-1-934774-15-1
ISBN-10: 1-934774-15-4

Edited by Donald A. Wood, Ph.D.
Essay by Ali Istalifi
Director's Foreword by Gail C. Andrews
Collector's Preface by Peggy Slappey
Curator's Introduction by Donald A. Wood, Ph.D.
Designed by James E. Williams
Photography by M. Sean Pathasema
    (unless otherwise noted)
Copy-edited and proofed by Caroline Wingate
Printed and bound by Walker 360

COVER: Cat. 14, detail

ENDPAPERS: *Soil Map of Uzbekskoi (Uzbekistan)*, details, 1960, Genusov, A.Z; Gorbunov, B.V.; Kimberg, N.V., General Directorate of Surveying and Cartography of the Soviet Ministry, GUGK, SSSR. Courtesy of the European Digital Archive of Soil Maps, European Commission.

The Birmingham Museum of Art gratefully acknowledges the generous support provided by the Robert R. Meyer Foundation, The E. Rhodes and Leona B. Carpenter Foundation, The Lydia Eustis Rogers Fund, the Alabama State Council on the Arts and the National Endowment for the Arts, and support from the City of Birmingham.

CONTENTS

DIRECTOR'S FOREWORD

GAIL C. ANDREWS
THE R. HUGH DANIEL DIRECTOR
BIRMINGHAM MUSEUM OF ART

The collection of Asian art at the Birmingham Museum of Art is one of our great strengths and offers a stellar representation of cultures from most of this vast area. However, textiles from Central Asia, particularly the rich and luxurious robes and accessories from Uzbekistan, are lacking in our holdings.

"All the colors of the rainbow" is how one early 19th-century diplomat described the ikat robes found in the bazaars and desert oases of Central Asia. Uzbekistan ikat robes and accessories, from the collection of Peggy Slappey, open a window into a culture and tradition that is not often seen in the West. A cooperative effort between people of different religions and backgrounds, the production of an ikat textile is a complex process that takes many skilled hands. From the raising of the silkworms to the final polishing of the material requires great effort and time.

We are delighted to show for the first time the wonderful array of Uzbekistan ikat robes and accessories from the collection of Peggy Slappey. Her keen eye and desire to learn and share have resulted in an exceptional selection. We are also grateful to her for including us in her estate planning. It is through such generosity and forethought that the collections at the Museum continue to grow in depth and quality.

This stunning exhibition offers the opportunity to better understand the rich culture of Uzbekistan's ikat tradition.

CAT. 27

CAT. 19

ACKNOWLEDGEMENTS

DONALD A. WOOD, PH.D.
SENIOR CURATOR
THE VIRGINIA AND WILLIAM M. SPENCER III CURATOR OF ASIAN ART
BIRMINGHAM MUSEUM OF ART

A project such as this involves many people to bring it to a successful conclusion. However, without the passion and vision of Peggy Slappey, none of this would be. Ms. Slappey has a great love for the arts, a strong desire to preserve and protect objects, and gets great joy from sharing her collections. Thank you, Peggy.

Gail Andrews, The R. Hugh Daniel Director of the Birmingham Museum of Art enthusiastically encouraged the project since she first saw one of the ikat robes. Ali Istalifi is a specialist in Central Asian textiles who lives in London. He kindly joined the project team. His family is from Kabul, where his father still lives. They have been involved with Central Asian textiles for several generations, and we are grateful for his essay and insights. Mary Dusenbury came to review the collection and share her considerable knowledge and insights as to the materials and construction involved, identification of each type of robe and approximate dates for the pieces. Howard Sutcliffe assessed the conservation needs of the collection, while our Objects Conservator, Margaret Burnham, and Collections Care Manager, Lisa Stewart, assisted with the careful cataloguing of the collection. The considerable task of photographing everything fell to our Director of Photography and Visual Services, Sean Pathasema. Creative Director, James Williams, did an outstanding job with the catalogue layout and design, while Caroline Wingate carefully edited the catalogue. And, Senior Associate Registrar, Suzanne Stephens had infinite patience in tracking down the various copyrights and rights of reproductions needed for the project.

Other BMA staff who assisted so ably include:

Horace Ballard	Terry Beckham	Cate Boehm
Ellen Ezekiel	Kristen Greenwood	Meghan Ann Hellenga
Alex McClurg	Joe McCreary	Kristi McMillan
Eric McNeal	Nathan Poe	Lindsey Reynolds
Rebecca Schaller	Spencer Shoults	Suzi Van Sickle Richey
Kristi Taft	Priscilla Tapio	Rose Wood

And finally to our sponsors; grants from the Robert R. Meyer Foundation, the E. Rhodes and Leona B. Carpenter Foundation, The Lydia Eustis Rogers Fund, the Alabama State Council on the Arts and the National Endowment for the Arts, and support from the City of Birmingham made this all possible.

My thanks to everyone.

THE ALLURE
OF ADORNMENT

PEGGY SLAPPEY

It was Ramadan 1997 when I boarded a plane in Nairobi, Kenya, to Peshawar, Pakistan. Of course I was quite nervous; however, I would go anywhere if it were a mission to collect rare art. As I come from the deep south of Georgia, I knew this would be different as soon as I stepped onto the Pakistani Airways flight from Dubai on to Peshawar. It was impossible not to be noticed, as I was the only woman on a flight full of Muslim men returning from their long awaited and precious trek to Mecca. I was enthralled with everything around me. All the men with their long beards, prayer beads, and traditional dress were quietly lost in their serenity and devotion. Every so often they would come out of their seats, lay down their prayer rugs and pray. One after another did this, but it wasn't until the pilot came out and unrolled his prayer rug for prayers that my heart skipped a beat.

We arrived in Peshawar with its tiny airport full of joyful relatives and villagers who along with their animals turned out to welcome these men from their holy trek. It was all so loud as the chatter and hugs went on and on. When the luggage came out it consisted of my suitcase and container after container of holy water, the only thing they brought back. As I looked around me at all the love and joyfulness my whole body suddenly shuddered with the realization that something wonderful was about to happen inside me. Thus was the beginning of my love affair with Central Asian textiles.

Peshawar was an ancient city not much different from 2,000 years ago when Christ walked the earth. I loved its rich textures and its beautifully exotic people. It never failed to excite me when I would see some rugged dark skinned man with startling sky blue eyes from Alexander the Great. I was a starving girl and did not know it. Peshawar proved to be a cultural feast.

I stayed near the refugee camp right by the markets. Every day for four weeks I would put on a traditional dress and head cover and venture out. It was obvious to anyone I was an outsider, with my long red hair sticking out from my head cover and a look of a deer in headlights, but I learned a long time ago that the most important thing I put on every day was a smile on my face. That and a keen awareness of my surroundings, as well as looking people in the eye with the utmost respect. All served me well as all the shopkeepers were wonderful to me. They would answer my probing questions with patience and if it was lunchtime I was always invited to their homes as an honored guest. I saw very few women out on the streets, but if I did they were covered from head to toe with a thin veil over their faces. The wives and children in the shopkeepers' homes did not speak a word of English. None was needed, as their kindness was so apparent.

CAT. 25

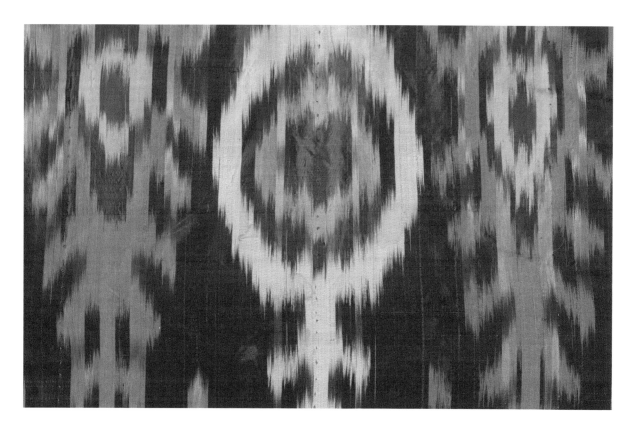

CAT. 16

What I saw in those markets that struck me to the core were their amazing textiles. The *suzanis* with tiny stitched birds and flowers that took years to produce, many begun when a girl child was born. These were the wedding bedcovers with many other types of embroideries all done by hand. There were the robes done in embroidery all from different tribal groups. However, the robes that struck me as the most powerful reminders of times past were the ikat *chapans*. The dyes and patterns were astounding works of art. Each had a different cotton lining with huge patterns and bright colors. I knew it would take me years to learn and discover more and more of the fantastic stories they would tell. I did manage to buy some extraordinary things before I left Peshawar. However, the main thing I left with was a realization of how little I knew. I was fortunate to find a friend like Ali Istalifi who has taught me most of what I now know about Central Asian textiles.

There are always those who would destroy their precious things that they wear and cook in, their customs and celebrations of life and its passages, their temples and holy places. My hope is that we can open our eyes to our differences that make us authentic, courageous human beings. However, there will also be people and institutions like the Birmingham Museum of Art who treasure the bygone eras and cultures we may never see again. We preserve them for those who come after us, who will never know there were once the most beautiful silk robes made by hand and worn like royalty in the deserts of a faraway land.

INTRODUCTION

DONALD A. WOOD, PH.D.
SENIOR CURATOR
THE VIRGINIA AND WILLIAM M. SPENCER III CURATOR OF ASIAN ART
BIRMINGHAM MUSEUM OF ART

Ifirst met Peggy Slappey with my colleague Dr. Emily Hanna when we were encouraged by textile conservator Howard Sutcliffe to visit Ms. Slappey to see her collections. We called, set up an appointment for March 7, 2013, and made the pleasant drive to Ms. Slappey's home in Georgia. What a surprise! Ms. Slappey was a bundle of wonderful, fun energy who greeted us at the front door and then welcomed us into her treasure house. Wonders were everywhere, and what wonders! African textiles and beadwork, textiles from all over Central Asia, Chinese jades, Thai sculpture, puppets, jewelry, hats, rugs—and that just scratched the surface.

Ms. Slappey brought out several prized pieces to share with us, in both African and Central Asian material. Beautiful African beadwork, which she subsequently loaned to the Museum, and wonderful ikat robes from Uzbekistan that immediately caught my attention. All the colors of the rainbow! She began to unpack robe after robe, each more beautiful than the last. And then came hats and jewelry, as well. She was knowledgeable about each piece, its history, its use, and how it was made. She had read and studied much of the available written material and was eager to talk about each piece. I was a total novice in textile history and design, but the beautiful materials she had to share captivated me.

We immediately hit upon the idea of an exhibition. After discussions here at the Museum, we made a return visit to Ms. Slappey's in July of that year and began to borrow pieces for the exhibition, *All the Colors of the Rainbow*. Subsequent visits over the next year resulted in our borrowing 26 ikat robes, plus hats, boots, bags, jewelry, and wall hangings.

Modern Uzbekistan includes many of the great cities of the ancient Silk Road. It has been an important crossroad for trade for centuries. The area that is now Uzbekistan was once part of the ancient Persian Empire and later part of the Turkic Khaganate and the Timurid Empire. The area was gradually incorporated into the Russian Empire in the 19th century. In 1921 it became a constituent republic of the Soviet Union and in 1991, after the collapse of the Soviet Union, was declared the Republic of Uzbekistan.

Such names as Samarkand, Bukhara, and Tashkent conjure up romantic images of lush ancient oases and great cities within Uzbekistan, with thriving markets filled with goods from all over the known world. First called the Silk Road by the German geographer Ferdinand von Richthofen (1833–1905), these routes show evidence of trade for at least the past 2,000 years. There is no one specific road that is the Silk Road, and no one known person traversed the entire length of the many paths that fan out across Central Asia to connect the great domains that flourished at important junctures. The trade routes were often changing, according to the ebb and flow of peoples and politics.

The very term "Silk Road" defines one of the principal goods carried through Central Asia from China to the Mediterranean Sea: silk. Used as currency and a luxury good, literally millions of bolts of silk changed hands over the centuries. Relatively lightweight, easy to transport and desirable, silk was a staple product of trade.

Silk production was an ancient tradition in Uzbekistan. However robes made of silk did not develop into a rainbow of colors until sometime in the early 19th century, long after the Silk Road was a viable trade entity. Red, green, yellow, purple, blue, pink, almost every color imaginable, are found in the ikat robes produced in this area at this time. These were used as clothing, decoration, and gifts.

Ikat is a technique used to pattern textiles that employs a resist dyeing process similar to tie-dye on either the warp or weft fibers, prior to weaving. Warp is the set of lengthwise threads attached to a loom, while weft is the thread that is drawn through the warp threads to create cloth. Greasy thread bindings, which resist dye penetration, are applied to the threads in the desired patterns and the threads are then dyed. Alteration of the bindings and the dyeing of more than one color produce elaborate, multicolored patterns. When all of the dyeing is finished the bindings are removed and the threads are ready to be woven into cloth. The resulting cloth is then made into beautiful robes that are a vibrant combination of colors.

The making of ikat begins with the production of silk. Women raised the silkworms that spun the cocoons that were then sold in the bazaars to men. The men then unwound the cocoons into thread, dyed the threads, and finally wove the cloth. A set division of labor among a variety of specialized craftsmen from the Jewish and Arab communities was involved in this complex process.

The name ikat comes from the Malaysian word *menjikat* (to tie). This complex dyeing technique developed independently in several parts of the world; Latin America, Japan, Indonesia, India, and western Central Asia are among the most important.

Clothing showed rank and status in the oasis communities. The wealthiest people wore the costly bright silk ikats, while those in lesser positions wore similar robes, but made of cotton. Nineteenth-century photographs of Central Asia show that men, women, and children all dressed in this finery. Ikats were a commodity of the great bazaars. As such, the active trade in these robes meant they were available and appreciated by various peoples of the steppes.

The Museum has hosted and originated many exhibitions concerning various aspects of Asian art over the years, but never one about Central Asia and certainly not one about Uzbekistan. We are proud to expand our horizons and to present for the first time these wonderful treasures from the collection of Peggy Slappey. We are also very grateful to Ms. Slappey for the promise of future gifts in her estate planning.

MAP OF UZBEKISTAN

1

CENTRAL ASIAN IKATS

ALI ISTALIFI

Imagine a society where silk covered almost everything: its population wearing colorful, mystically designed dresses, hats, and robes; its homes hung with intricately embroidered tapestries; and even its horses and camels covered with polychrome stitched trappings. You have imagined the Central Asian cities of the 19th and early 20th centuries.

The region produced some of the most beautiful and sophisticated silk fabrics in history. Of all their textiles, the dazzling silk ikats—bold and visually mesmerizing—were among the most coveted.

In the world of textile collecting, ikat is the term for most woven cotton and/or silk textiles that use resist dye techniques to achieve their patterns. The word is derived from an Indonesian Malay language term meaning to bind or to tie.

Ikat production has not been restricted to Central Asia. The tradition has also existed in the rest of Asia and beyond. In fact, it can be argued that the resist dye or tie-dye technique is one of the oldest forms of textile production and that the tradition developed in some form in most cultures across the globe during different eras.

Examples of such textiles can be seen in cultures as far apart as Central and South America, Africa, South Asia, and Southeast Asia. But Central Asian ikat textiles stand apart; with their powerful designs in bold and saturated colors, they can be dazzling spectacles of textile art.

THE RISE AND DEMISE OF THE CENTRAL ASIAN IKAT MARKET

The tradition of ikat production in Central Asia is strongly linked to the cultural history of its people, the economic fluctuations their lands experienced, and the geopolitical changes, particularly during the 19th and 20th centuries A look at the history of these people can help us understand the rise and demise of their ikat tradition—and how these fabrics captured the imagination of collectors and museums around the world.

The map of pre-Soviet Central Asia was quite different from today's. The current borders exist because Russia took control of Uzbekistan, Turkmenistan, Tajikistan, Kyrgyzstan, and Kazakhstan in the late 19th century and, after the 1917 Bolshevik Revolution, divided them into separate Socialist republics.

Thus the current borders can wrongly suggest that ethnic Uzbek people must have all lived in Uzbekistan, Turkmens in Turkmenistan, Kyrgyz people in Kyrgyzstan, Tajiks in Tajikistan, and Kazakhs in Kazakhstan. But this simple concept does not represent the complex ethnic makeup of this area.

The period photographs in the catalogue come from two sources.

TURKESTAN ALBUM

Contains over 1200 gold-toned albumen photographic prints and was published in 1872 by order of the first Governor-General of Russian Turkestan, Konstantin Petrovich Von Kaufman (1818–1882). It was designed to familiarize Russian and western researchers with the Turkestan region. One of three known sets is at the Library of Congress and is reproduced with their permission.

PROKUDIN-GORSKII COLLECTION

Contains several thousand images of the Russian Empire made between 1905 and 1915. The photographer, Sergei Mikhaylovich Prokudin-Gorskii (1863–1944), was the first to use the three-color principle in photographs of Russia. With this principle three photographs of the same scene are taken with three colored filters (red, green and blue). When superimposed on top of each other a full color image results. The images reproduced are with permission of the Library of Congress.

FIG. I On the Registan, Samarkand, LC-DIG-prokc-21726

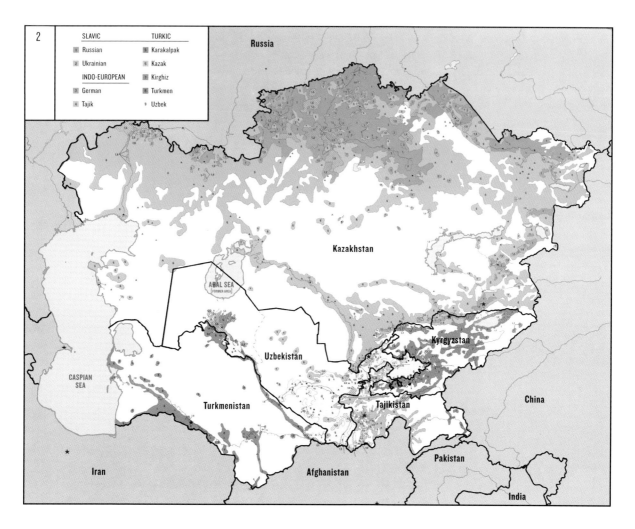

During the 19th century, when Central Asian people had more autonomy, the main ethnic groups were Uzbek, Turkmen, Tajik, Kyrgyz, and Kazakh, plus a number of smaller tribes [FIG. 2]. Going slightly south, these ethnic groups spilled over into Afghanistan, living alongside Pashtun tribes and Baloch people, and on the east they spilled over into the Xinjiang region of western China, where they resided alongside the Uighur people.

This region was a collection of desert oasis kingdoms, or khanates, situated at the heart of the Silk Road, the ancient trade routes that connected East Asia and the Mediterranean Sea [FIG. 3]. Some of these khanates grew into large cities with their rule expanding to the surrounding rural villages. The largest and most famous of these cities were Bukhara, Samarkand, Khwarezm, Khiva, Fergana, and Shakhrisabz. For centuries, the growing wealth of these khanates was rooted to their location on the Silk Road. The caravans of merchants carrying spices, precious metal, handicrafts, and silks brought prosperity and turned their main cities into important trade centers.

In the late 18th and early 19th centuries, the city of Bukhara was experiencing a flourishing economy. With this wealth a lavishly spending society emerged, luxuriously decorating their homes and wearing expensive silk garments and jewelry. The growing demand for textiles ignited a boom in silk production that paved the way for a rich tradition of colorful silk embroidery (often referred to as *suzani*), silk embroidered decorations for homes, and delicately stitched and woven silk garments (hats, hair covers, belts, trousers, robes, dresses, and shirts). So much silk was manufactured during this period that these people even dressed their horses and camels with lavishly embroidered silks. This demand for silk textiles fueled the rise of ikat production.

Even though Central Asian people had been making ikats for centuries, it was only during the economic boom of the 19th century that the art really exploded. There was a growth in the number of workshops and increasing innovation of design, color, and

FIG. 2 Major ethnic groups in Central Asia, based on map created by the Central Intelligence Agency, 1992, Library of Congress Geography and Map Division, Washington, D.C., LC-92685272

FIG. 3 Map of the Silk Road

FIG. 4 Bukhara bureaucrat, Bukhara, LC-DIG-prokc-21884

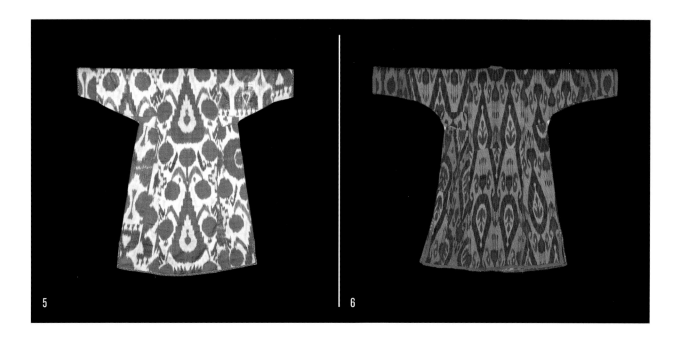

FIG. 5 Ikat robe, Bukhara, 19th century, Cat. 14

FIG. 6 Ikat robe, Fergana Valley, 19th century, Cat. 9

quality. Most antique ikat robes and hangings that we see today are from the 19th century, the golden era of ikat. These fabrics were not only used by the local population but were also exported to neighboring regions. Some of the more sophisticated examples were given by the kings or emirs to visiting foreign dignitaries.

Initially the main centers of ikat production were the khanates of Bukhara, Khwarezm, and Kokand. Their workshops, urban and rural, constantly pushed the boundaries of the craft to produce more elaborate designs with more extravagant colors. By the mid-19th century, Bukhara had become the largest producer of ikat fabrics. Samarkand and Kokand also produced a significant amount, but the innovation in design and color of the Bukhara examples was hard to match [FIG. 5].

Samarkand, once the capital of the Timurid Empire, had a healthy tradition of ikat production. Perhaps it was not as extensive as Bukhara, but because of the wealth of the city, the residents could afford it. But in the mid-19th century, Samarkand entered a gradual economic decline, and ikat production slowed drastically. By the end of the century, the few remaining workshops found it hard to compete with textiles imported from larger cities, resulting in the decline in the quantity and quality of their ikats. From then on most ikat fabrics would be imported from other cities, mainly Bukhara.

The Fergana Valley, on the other hand, was becoming another major center of ikat production in the second half of the 19th century. Its artisans started exploring designs and dye colors that were different from those of Bukhara and elsewhere. These designs, with more rustic blue and green hues [FIG. 6], contrasted strongly with the rich, vividly colored ikats of Bukhara.

7

By the end of the 19th century the Fergana Valley surpassed Bukhara in the output of ikat fabrics. While its workshops were not as sophisticated and lacked Bukhara's skilled master craftsmen, they out-produced everyone, mainly because Bukhara was sinking into recession. The production of its sophisticated ikats was so time consuming that its output was limited. Despite their higher quality fabrics, the workshops' income lagged behind. In addition, competition from lower quality silk ikats produced in smaller towns and an economic decline in the region due to the expansion of the Russian empire, meant that producing high-end ikat fabrics was far too costly. Many workshops closed down.

Fergana Valley workshops continued to produce, but eventually they, too, suffered the same financial turmoil. By the early 20th century most of these towns retained their territories only if they accepted Russian dominance, but their financial independence was lost and their economies damaged. Ikat production suffered, with many workshops turning to garments of cheap quality silks or even cotton.

Sociopolitical changes following the Bolshevik revolution and the Soviet invasion of Central Asia caused ikat production to die out, and also killed the quality of other textile traditions. The leaders of most khanates were killed or forced out; the emir of Bukhara, for example, fled to Afghanistan where he died in exile [FIG. 8].

The Soviet regime began restructuring the lifestyle of these once-independent people into one that would benefit the USSR. First, the Central Asian lands were divided by artificial borders, and in 1924 most of the ikat-producing cities such as Bukhara, Fergana, and Samarkand became part of what is now Uzbekistan.

FIG. 7 Samarkand bazaar and its types of vendors, market square between three madrasas (Registan), LC-DIG-ppmsca-12228

FIG. 8 Emir of Bukhara, Bukhara, LC-DIG-prokc-21887

Second, the regime found the region's unique cultural identity a threat to the ambitions of the Soviet Union. So these lands were forced to change their written language from Arabic to Cyrillic script. It has been suggested that the USSR felt its control of the region depended on dismantling the individual cultures, making them uniform. Inevitably the cultural output of the people suffered, particularly their textile tradition. As the population was mobilized to work in large industries and cotton production, there was no place in Soviet Central Asia for delicate and luxurious silk fabrics. Slowly ikat designs were incorporated into machine-made fabrics, and eventually the art died. By the second quarter of the 20th century, ikat production had ceased in Central Asia.

Many locals who fled communism went to neighboring countries such as Afghanistan, bringing with them their heirloom ikat fabrics. But as poor refugees, they didn't have the means or ability to restart ikat production. Uzbeks in northern Afghanistan near the city of Mazar-i-Sharif tried to restart ikat production during the second quarter of the 20th century. These workshops' main output was a copy of one 19th-century design, vertical bands repeating a triangular motif with comb-shaped edges. But this design was crudely interpreted with slightly coarse silks that didn't have the finesse of the older pieces. They produced many of these, seldom experimenting with other designs [FIGS. 9 & 10].

Finally, in the 1960s and 1970s, travelers from the West became fascinated by the rug and textile bazaars of Kabul. Some became rug and textile dealers, introducing these textiles to collectors, decorators, and textile aficionados in Europe, Japan, the United States, and elsewhere.

Perhaps it was the archaic designs or the psychedelic colors of these silk fabrics that captured the imagination of the West in the 1970s. Interest and demand for these textiles grew with every exhibition. Museums around the world began purchasing

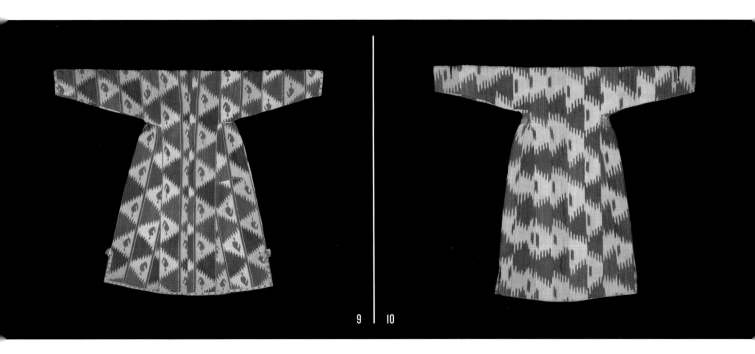

9 | 10

and exhibiting them, and by the 1980s Central Asian ikats of the 19th century were demanding high prices in international auction houses.

Most of these antique ikats were found in Afghanistan, having been brought there by the refugees from Soviet-invaded Central Asia. The children and grandchildren of these refugees would sell their textiles to local merchants who would take them to bigger dealers in Kabul, who sold the pieces to dealers and collectors in the West. Had these ikats not made their way to the West, they might have disintegrated, their beauty undiscovered.

With the Soviet invasion of Afghanistan and the subsequent civil war, the Afghan rug market shifted from Kabul to Peshawar, Pakistan. In the late 1980s and early 1990s Kabul was too dangerous for international dealers. Afghan refugees from war and invasion brought many of their textiles, including their ikats to Pakistan. Western dealers continued to purchase them via the Peshawar market. But soon all interesting surviving ikat fabrics in both Afghanistan and Pakistan were sold out.

In the early 1990s, after the fall of the Soviet Union, Uzbekistan and other Soviet republics became independent. Turkey was the first country to acknowledge their sovereignty, easing its visa restriction and allowing most Uzbeks to easily visit Turkey. This political move resulted in many people from Uzbekistan selling heirloom ikat textiles in the Istanbul rug bazaars. A number of unseen antique ikat textiles found their way to the Istanbul market during the 1990s and were sold to collectors from Europe, the United States, and Japan. Some of these ikats, along with ones purchased in the 1970s and 1980s in Kabul, helped form some of the most renowned collections in the world. Most of these collections were either donated or exhibited in some of the world's great museums. These ikats slowly became accepted as one of the most important, sophisticated and rich textile arts.

FIG. 9 Ikat robe, Central Asia, late 19th century, Cat. 2

FIG. 10 Ikat robe, Mazar-i-Sharif, first half 20th century, Cat. 3

THE INTRICATE PROCESS BEHIND IKAT FABRICS

Only when we explore the complex methods that produced ikat fabric can we appreciate the craftsmanship and artistry of this very rich textile tradition.

No ikat fabric was the work of an individual. No single person could master all the skills required. An ikat was the work of a number of artisans and technicians delivering each phase of the production. Every phase benefited from generations of experience.

The process began with the cultivation of silkworms on mulberry leaves [FIG. 11]. Once the silkworms began pupating in their cocoons, the cocoons would be immersed in boiling water; then the long fibers of raw silk would be extracted and spun onto spools [FIG. 12].

Considering the high number of fibers needed, the process was tedious and time consuming. This was perhaps why raw silk was valued as much as gold and other precious materials.

Several strands of the silk fibers would be spun together onto a reeling wheel to make threads that would either be sold for embroidery or made ready for the next phase of producing ikats [FIG. 13].

Meanwhile other technicians (often women) would be busy preparing the weft threads [FIG. 14]. The early ikats of Central Asia had cotton weft which would have been woven onto the patterned silk warp threads.

It was extremely difficult to weave ikats with silk wefts, and until the third quarter of the 19th century almost all ikats were silk warp with cotton weft. This type of ikat is known as *adras* weaving. By the end of the 19th century weavers had mastered intricate techniques that allowed them to weave silk wefts on silk warps. These pure silk ikats became known as *atlas* or *shahi*. The rule of thumb in identifying the age of ikats has often been that *adras* ikats are the same age or older than *atlas* ikats. The cotton wefts would be wound onto four or more sticks in the courtyard of the workshop. Often the less experienced weavers would be given the task of handling the cotton wefts as cotton was less expensive. Once they mastered their craft, they were promoted to handling the silk threads.

Those technicians responsible for handling the silks were busy preparing the warp. The threads would be spun on a larger reeling wheel and then stretched onto a vertically positioned spinning wheel. These two processes would produce silk threads of the uniform thickness necessary to sustain balance in the design [FIGS. 15 & 16].

Another technician would build the looms from reed and wood bought at the local market. The looms were often long and narrow approximatcly 10 to 20 inches wide and 13 to 16 feet long. The finished ikat fabric of these sizes would be cut up and stitched together to make garments and hangings. After the loom was prepared, the silk warp was threaded into it [FIGS. 17 & 18].

The next stage would be one of the most important in the whole production line. The *nishanzan* was the artist who drew the design of an ikat onto the silk warp threads prior to dyeing and weaving. It is difficult to know whether this craftsman's designs were his own or whether they were provided by workshop owners. Whether designer or artist, he would have been a senior and experienced member of the production line [FIG. 19].

The most complex and time-consuming stage was the process of tie-dyeing the warp threads. But before we explore it, we must understand the tradition of dye making in the region. An essential characteristic of 19th-century Central Asian weaving was its use of beautiful natural dyes. Producing the dyes was an art in itself, a talent usually passed down from parents and grandparents along with their closely guarded secrets for creating specific hues and saturations of color. Most of the dye makers were from the Central Asian Jewish community, especially in Bukhara.

However, there was a general knowledge of how most dyes were created. For instance, magenta came from the cochineal insect. Yellow was derived from delphinium. Mixed with copper, this yellow would produce a bright green, and mixed with iron, a brownish green. The sharp reds were derived from madder. Pomegranate skin with iron would produce strong black dyes. Indigo from India was one of the few dyes imported.

With these dyes at their disposal, the tie-dye process would begin. The loom was set at an angle of 45 or 30 degrees to help ease the weaving process [FIG. 20]. The design was incorporated onto the textile by tying parts of the warp (and sometimes parts of the weft) with oiled cotton. When the thread was dipped into the dye, the exposed areas absorbed the colors. Then the dyer removed the cotton and tied it onto another section of the threads, exposing another area to be dipped onto a different color dye. The process continued until each thread absorbed the necessary colors. Once the warp was dyed, the weft threads would be woven into the warp. When we consider the varied colors of each warp thread, we can realize the intricacy required to prevent ruining the design. Any slight adjustment of the threads would misalign the design.

The mathematical precision and delicate touch needed to produce a length of ikat was phenomenal. Every stage of production had to coordinate meticulously or the design would not work. No mistakes could be made at any phase. Even the simplest design was painstakingly woven thread by thread. Thus it makes sense that complex designs consisting of five or seven colors (known as *painjrang* or *haftrang adras*) were always the most coveted. The five- to seven-color ikats were often made by the best artisans in the most prestigious workshops. Their fabrics were often commissioned by the elite, including the aristocracy [FIG. 21].

21

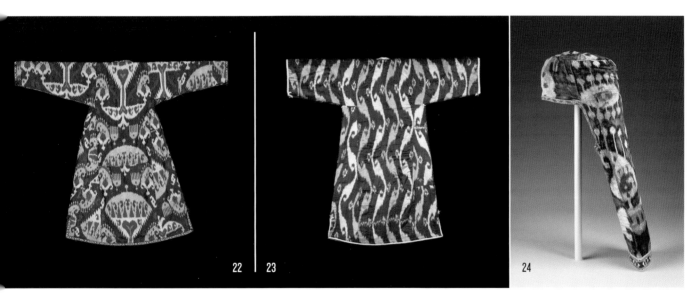

22 | 23

24

There were four forms of ikat fabrics. The older examples with silk warp and cotton weft were *adras* ikats. The older ikats generally had cotton wefts because the workshops had not learned to weave entirely with silk. The second was *atlas* or *shahi* ikats, with both warp and weft of silk. This tradition developed in the last quarter of the 19th century and continued until the early 20th century [FIG. 22]. The third was silk satin, which had a slightly shinier surface and was produced at the end of the 19th century but mostly in the early 1900s [FIG. 23]. The final form was the silk velvet ikat known as Bakhmal [FIG. 24], considered the most expensive and greatest of Central Asian ikats. The velvet ikat was made exclusively for the wealthy. The velvet ikat tradition lasted for only 25 to 30 years, which explains their rarity.

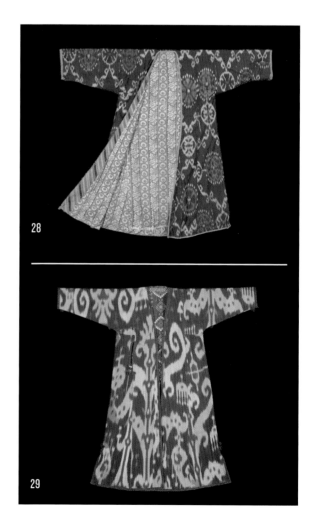

FIG. 25 Uzbek woman, LC-DIG-ppmsca-12187

FIG. 26 Central Asian boy, LC-DIG-ppmsca-14720

FIG. 27 Fabric printing production, printing patterns on the cloth, LC-DIG-ppmsca-14937

FIG. 28 Ikat Robe with Russian chintz lining, Fergana Valley or Samarkand, late 19th century, Cat. 24

FIG. 29 Ikat *chapan* with ribbed surfaced silk, Bukhara, second half 19th century, winter coat, Cat. 15

OTHER IKAT GARMENTS AND ACCESSORIES

Despite their beauty, at core ikats were functional fabrics. They were primarily made into robes called *chapans*. But they were also made into dresses, hats, wall hangings, padded bed covers, bags, purses, and linings for embroideries such as *suzani* hangings or brocade robes or belts.

The *chapans* were made for men and women, young and old [FIG. 25 & 26]. Lengths of ikat fabrics were displayed in bazaars where locals would buy from the shop keepers or commission the workshops to produce for them. Each region could be defined by the shape of its tailoring.

An ikat *chapan,* once tailored, would be lined with cotton. In the first half of the 19th century, most lining fabrics were made locally. These were often hand-woven cotton with block-print design [FIG. 27]. But after mid-century, Russian chintz fabrics were imported primarily as lining for *chapans* [FIG. 28].

These garments were worn daily. It is impossible not to be fascinated by a society dressed in such ikats with their bold colors and psychedelic designs. Some *chapans* were made with a ribbed texture created by lines of stitching about a half inch apart. Often a layer of cotton padding was inserted between the ikat and its lining, creating a winter coat [FIG. 29].

Ikat was just one of many rich fabrics that the Central Asian people wore. Often these lavish textiles were paired with brocades or extravagant gold- or silver-embroidered silk garments. Men wore leather or velvet boots with intricate floral embroideries in silks or silver and gold metal work [FIGS. 30 & 31].

Their other accessories could include silver belts, brocade *chapans* over ikat *chapans,* and silk-embroidered hats and caps [FIGS. 32 & 33]. For both men and boys, the hat was a vital part of the costume; each region and ethnic group had its distinct hat, defined by embroidered motifs and stitching.

FIG. 30 Boots, silk embroidered leather, Central Asia, early 20th century, Cat. 41

FIG. 31 Boots, silver embroidered velvet, Bukhara, late 19th century, Cat. 42

FIG. 32 Cap, silk embroidered, Uzbekistan, early 20th century, Cat. 36

FIG. 33 Cap, silk embroidered, Uzbekistan, early 20th century, Cat. 37

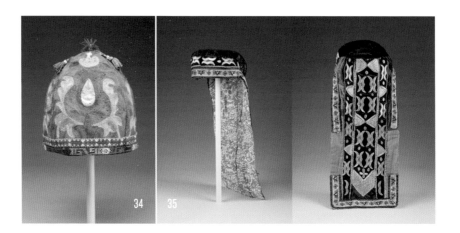

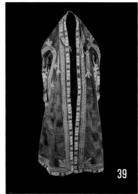

The accessories that women wore with their ikat garments included extravagant silk- and silver-embroidered hats with embroidered or silver-appliquéd hats with long pockets, or *kultas*, at the back to hold their braided hair. Each region had its own style. Bukhara women often wore velvet hats with silver or gilded silver embroidery, while the hats of women of Shakhrisabz were often silk embroidered with lovely floral designs [FIGS. 34 & 35].

When women wore their complete outfits including the ikat dresses, ikat *chapans*, the hair pieces and shawls, the effect was both beautiful and dramatic [FIGS. 36, 37, & 38].

Outside the home and in the presence of others, women wore a *paranja* or *faranji*. While this large garment looked like a coat with very long sleeves, it was worn over the head. The false sleeves were there for decoration. The *paranja* was often monochrome silk, velvet, or cotton with delicate silk embroidery on the edges. The best examples were lined with the finest ikat fabrics [FIGS. 39 & 40].

When it came to jewelry and accessories, there was a significant difference in style and the type of things each ethnic group wore. For instance while the Uzbek groups wore simple tasselled veils [FIG. 41], Turkmen, Kazakh, and Karakalpak women often wore much more elaborate headgear sometimes with gilded silver work and carnelian stone work.

Turkmen tribes in particular had a rich tradition of jewelry. Women would often dress in archaic and lavish gilded silver with carnelian inset jewelry. They had extravagant and large crowns known as *gupba* headgear and necklaces known as *bukov* that resembled dog collars because of their shape and thickness [FIGS. 42 & 43].

The number of uses for ikat fabrics was endless. The more expensive multicolored and uniquely designed examples often became beautiful robes. Lesser quality ikats would be used as lining for other expensive textiles, such as embroideries or gold- and silver-embroidered garments.

Since the major function of ikat fabrics was to make robes, it follows that the type of *chapan* worn represented the social status of the wearer. For example, the aristocracy often wore the most unusual and intricately made *chapans* of velvet ikat. Government officials or ministers were also defined by their ikat robes. Even religion was announced by the type of ikat a person wore. So garments, ikat or other types, were signatures of one's pedigree. The same went for the accessories.

FIG. 34 Hat, silk embroidered, Shakhrisabz, early 20th century, Cat. 40

FIG. 35 Hat, gold embroidered on velvet, Bukhara, late 19th century, Cat. 31

FIGS. 36, 37 & 38 Central Asian women, LC-DIG-ppmsca-14431, 14429, and 14428

FIG. 39 *Paranja* or *faranji* cloak, Uzbekistan, late 19th–early 20th century, Cat. 26

FIG. 40 Tajik wedding, meeting of the bride with the groom, [Women covering themselves under *paranja* or *faranji* cloaks], LC-DIG-ppmsca-14443

FIG. 41 Tasseled veil, Uzbekistan, early 20th century, Cat. 34

FIG. 42 *Gupba* hat, Central Asia, early 20th century, Cat. 29

FIG. 43 *Bukov* necklace, Central Asia, early 20th century, Cat. 45

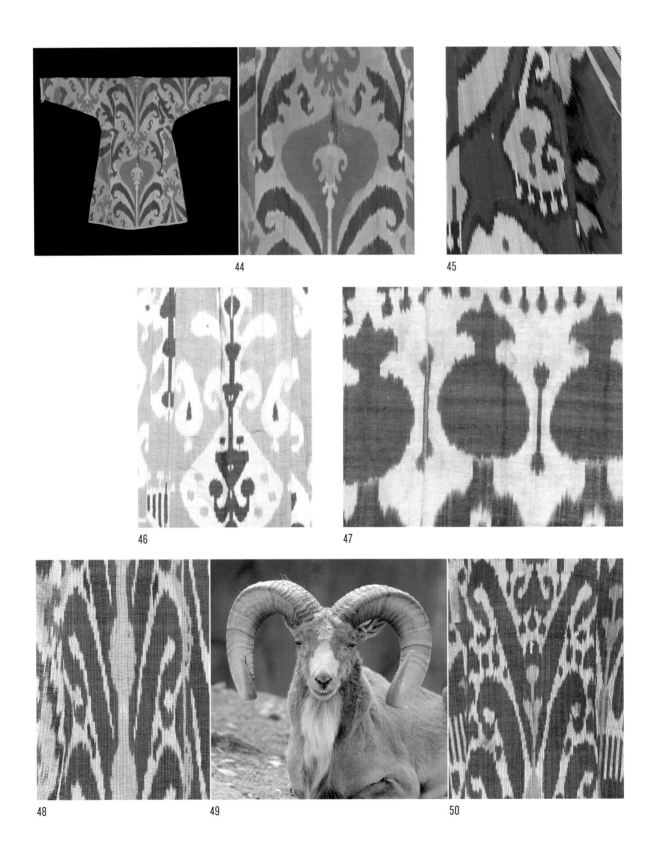

44

45

46

47

48 49 50

THE LANGUAGE BEHIND THE ENIGMATIC DESIGNS OF THE IKATS

The word *abr*, meaning cloud, is often used to describe ikat patterns. These designs do somewhat resemble the enigmatic shapes of clouds, and the idea that nature inspired them is a plausible one. Many ikat weavers in Central Asia also suggest that their designs were based on the shapes formed by dropping oil into a bowl of water. Others suggest that the enigmatic shapes were less a language than a mystical expression. But one must wonder whether the designs speak a deeper language with roots in the ancient history of the region. To answer this question we must explore the historical relationship between pattern and textile.

The earliest human beings made clothes from animal hide or primitive textiles and wore them to cover themselves and keep warm. Textiles and weaving functioned only to serve this basic human need. As human social structures advanced, people started printing and drawing shapes on their garments, textiles, and other functional objects. This was done not necessarily for decoration; these designs were motifs rooted to their beliefs. At core the simplest designs were symbols and addressed desires for prosperity, fertility, and protection.

When children came of age, parents would teach them to make garments and put the symbolic motifs on them. But with every passing generation, the design of these symbols would evolve, reinterpreted into more elaborate versions of the original shapes. Over centuries, the meaning of these motifs was lost, and they would be seen simply as designs to beautify objects.

Looking at design from this perspective, we can see that the connecting of motifs within the context of history can give us an insight on the origin of a design. For instance, older items would often have more archaic and less busy designs, while the later designs would be more elaborate and detailed. This method doesn't necessarily decipher the exact language of an enigmatic design, but it can at least give us an idea.

There has always been imagery of flowers and vegetation in Central Asian ikats. These designs on a young woman's clothes were symbols of fertility, placed there with the hope she would have children and continue the family's line and the tribe's prosperity. Flowers were often seen in almost all forms of Central Asian textiles. Two especially strong nature motifs are the *boteh* (bud) and the leaf (which resembles paisley). The bud and the leaf are the quintessential imagery of fertility [FIGS. 44, 45, & 46].

The pomegranate, one of the common fruits in Central Asia, often appeared in ikat design, incorporated within the larger pattern [FIG. 47].

As for the protective motifs, one can suggest that they were there to ward off the evil eye or any other potential dangers. These protective motifs varied, depending on the tribe and its beliefs. As the cultures advanced, their protective symbols became more complex. In Central Asia one common protective motif is the ram's horn. This symbol is rooted to the shamanistic pre-Islamic history of the region. Its exact origin is not known. But perhaps early cultures saw the ram, living on the mountain, close to the heavens, as the animal with protective divine powers in its ultimate weapon, its horns. Therefore putting the ram's horn onto their garments would somehow protect them from danger. Another interpretation is that the ram is male and the protector of its herd. The motif often appeared as a repeating pattern of two curing shapes [FIGS. 48, 49, & 50].

FIG. 44 Ikat robe, *boteh* motif, Bukhara, second half 19th century, Cat.23

FIGS. 45 Ikat robe, leaf motif, Bukhara, second half 19th century, Cat. 22

FIG. 46 Ikat robe, leaf motif, Uzbekistan, second half 19th century, Cat. 5

FIG. 47 Ikat robe, pomegranate motif, Bukhara, second half 19th century, Cat. 1

FIG. 48 Ikat robe, ram's horn motif, Khwarezm, second half 19th century, Cat. 8

FIG. 49 A Transcaspian Urial
© Robin Winkelman | Dreamstime.com

FIG. 50 Ikat robe, ram's horn motif, Khwarezm, 19th century, Cat. 6

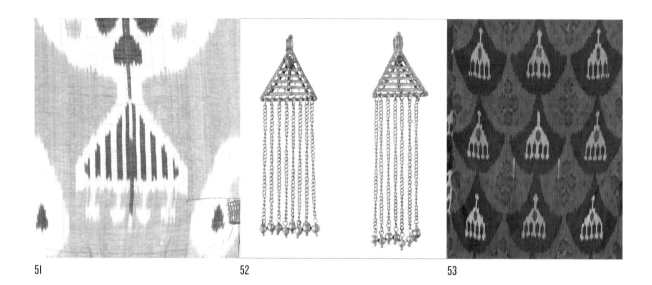

51   52   53

FIG. 51 Ikat robe, *moska* motifs, Uzbekistan, second half 19th century, Cat. 5

FIG. 52 *Moska* earrings, Central Asia, early 20th century, Cat. 52

FIG. 53 Ikat robe, *moska* motifs, Uzbekistan, late 19th century, Cat. 18

FIGS. 54 Ikat robe, *adamlyk* motif, Uzbekistan, second half 19th century, Cat. 5

FIG. 55 *Adamlyk* pendant, Central Asia, late 19th century, Cat. 46

FIG. 56 Animal skin illustration based on Tibetan design motifs

FIG. 57 Ikat robe, animal skin motif, Bukhara, second half 19th century, Cat. 13

Another strong influence on ikat designs was Central Asia's rich jewelry tradition. Often designers would draw motifs from the shapes that existed in silver and gilded silver jewelry. These jewelry pieces were three dimensional objects in the shapes of ancient symbolic motifs of Central Asian cultures. For example, triangular silver amulets with multiple long tassels known as *moska* often appear in ikat design. The *moska* was a symbol of protection. Its shape represented the dome top of the yurt, the circular tent in which most nomadic Central Asian people lived. By placing a symbol of the home, a place of protection, on jewelry or textiles, the wearer would receive the protection of the home [FIGS. 51, 52, 53].

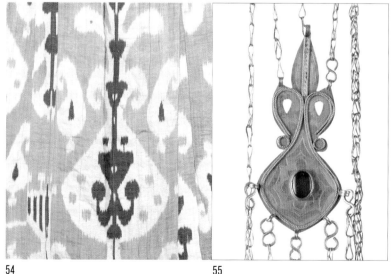

54   55

Another interesting type of jewelry was the *adamlyk,* a silver piece that would be hung on each side of the bridal hat. The *adamlyk* shape often appeared in ikat designs [FIGS. 54 & 55]. It resembles the Mother Goddess motif, which was common in many cultures. The exact root of this motif is difficult to pinpoint. But it was apparent in Hindu theology as well as Hellenistic cultures that existed in Central Asia after the conquest of these lands by Alexander the Great.

Central Asian designs were not solely rooted in local culture. Along with influences from other countries, design elements also arrived via the Silk Road. In Tibet there was a tradition of weaving rugs with designs depicting the hide of a tiger or other animal. Animal hides as design motifs were also common in Mongolian cultures and many regions of Southeast Asia [FIG. 56]. Central Asian cultures used animal hide, but as a design element it was rare. But one ikat motif may represent animal skin and must have come from neighboring cultures [FIG. 57]. The circular inner detail represents the sun (symbolizing fertility), and the purple and black design around it looks like the skin of an animal, a symbol of strength and protection.

The sources that influenced and/or inspired the designs of Central Asian ikats are endless and a much larger study is required to explore the subject. But one thing is certain: there is a deep symbolic language expressing cultural beliefs and superstitions. Perhaps this explains why ikat designs are so engaging, even to those unfamiliar with the genre. Speaking with thousands of years of symbolic languages, these designs inform the viewer on a level deeper than beauty alone. Considering the number of times that Central Asian civilizations have developed and fallen, by conquest or by influence, it is inevitable that the culture would get richer and the symbolic languages deeper and more sophisticated.

THE REVIVAL AND FUTURE OF IKAT WEAVING

As fascination with Central Asia's 19th-century ikats grew, prices skyrocketed and supplies dwindled. In the late 1990s and early 2000s, textile dealers and non-governmental organizations undertook initiatives to revive ikat production in Uzbekistan.

The task was difficult; it had been almost a hundred years since the tradition died. Uzbeks had forgotten the craft. But the study of ikats had been intense, producing enough references and material to begin the process of learning and reproducing.

In the early 2000s, workshops in rural Bukhara, Samarkand, and Tashkent region, through trial and error, learned to reproduce ikat textiles. They managed to replicate the dyes, the weave, and the designs to near 19th-century standards. The dyes were a bit off compared to older examples, and the weave was a touch looser, but nevertheless they were impressive. They exploded onto the international market, and decorators and designers around the world purchased them. They were cheaper than antique examples and somewhat echoed the beauty of the older ikats. Now it is a growing industry and impressively revived. Although the new production is more a commercial textile than an ethnographic or a folk art, they are as beautiful as the older pieces.

Over the last few years and following the global economic recession and an increase in silk prices in Central Asia, the production of new ikat fabrics has slowed. Without international support or commerce it is hard to predict whether the market will grow or once again gradually diminish.

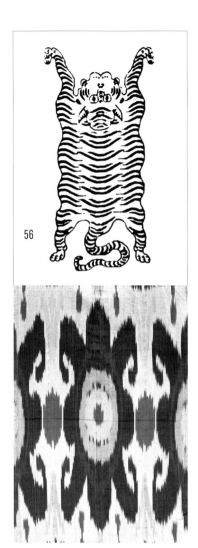

56

57

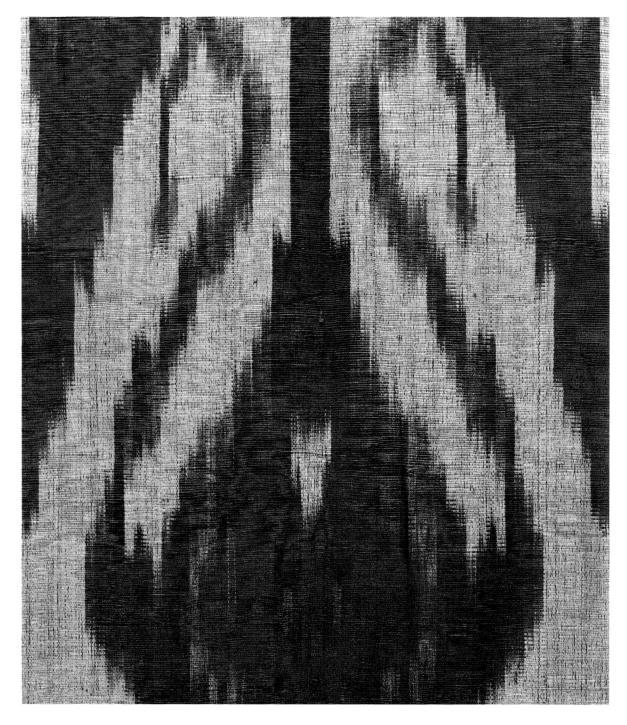

CAT. 21

BIBLIOGRAPHY

The following publications are available in the Clarence B. Hanson, Jr. Library at the Birmingham Museum of Art.

Amstey, Marvin S., Frederica Amstey, and George W. O'Bannon. 1990. *Vanishing Jewels: Central Asian Tribal Weavings: A Catalog of an Exhibition by the Rochester Museum & Science Center, September 14, 1990 to March 17, 1991 from the Collection of Marvin and Frederica Amstey*. Rochester, N.Y.: The Center.

Benardout, Raymond. 2002. *A Catalogue of Turkoman and Beluch Weavings from a Bygone Era*. Los Angeles, California: Raymond Benardout Gallery.

Browne, Clare Woodthorpe. 1989. *Ikats*. New York: H.N. Abrams.

Fitz Gibbon, Kate, and Andrew Hale. 1997. *Ikat: Silks of Central Asia : the Guido Goldman collection*. London: Laurence King in association with Alan Marcuson.

Kokusai Kirisutokyo Daigaku. 1993. *Indoneshia no Kasuri: Oda Korekushon ni Yoru = Indonesian Ikats from the Oda Collection*. Tokyo: Kokusai Kirisutokyo Daigaku Yuasa Hachiro Kinenkan.

Schletzer, Dieter, and Reinhold Schletzer. 1983. *Old Silver Jewellery of the Turkoman: An Essay on Symbols in the Culture of Inner Asian Nomads*. Berlin: D. Reimer.

Sodiqova, Nafisa. 2006. *National Uzbek Clothes of Tashkent and Fergana, XIX-XX Centuries*. Tashkent: "Shark".

Textile Museum (Washington, D.C.), Sumru Belger Krody, and Feza Çakmut. 2010. *Colors of the Oasis: Central Asian Ikats*. Washington, D.C.: Textile Museum.

Tomita, Jun, and Noriko Tomita. 1982. *Japanese Ikat Weaving: the Techniques of Kasuri*. London: Routledge & Kegan Paul.

The Library also has many issues of the magazine *Hali: Carpet, Textile and Islamic Art* from 1978 on.

CAT. I

WOMAN'S ROBE

Second half 19th century
Central Asia, Uzbekistan, Bukhara
Silk warp, glazed cotton weft,
Russian roller print cotton interior
T.2014.570

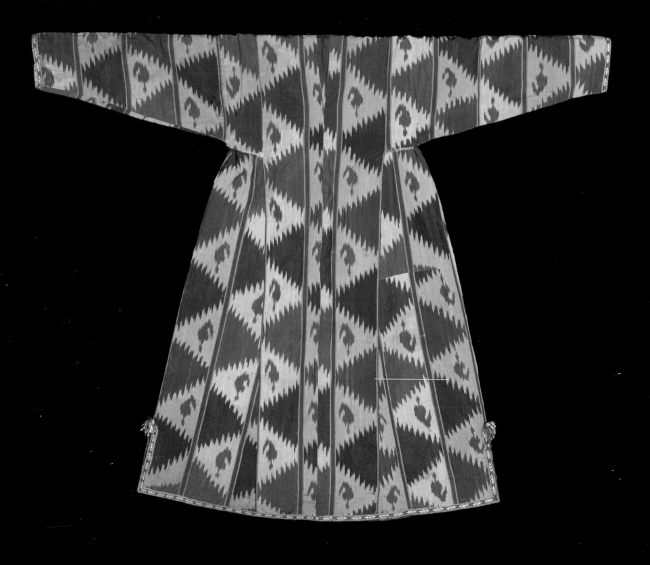

CAT. 2

WOMAN'S ROBE

Late 19th century
Central Asia, Uzbekistan
Silk warp and weft *shahi* ikat,
Russian roller print cotton interior
83.2013

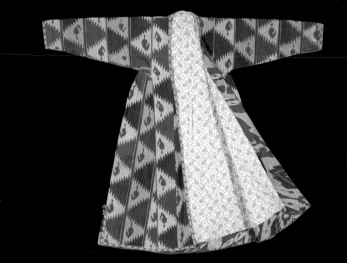

CAT. 3

WOMAN'S ROBE

Mid 20th century
Central Asia, Afghanistan, Mazar-i-Sharif
Silk warp and weft, woven plaid interior
and roller printed cloth
79.2013

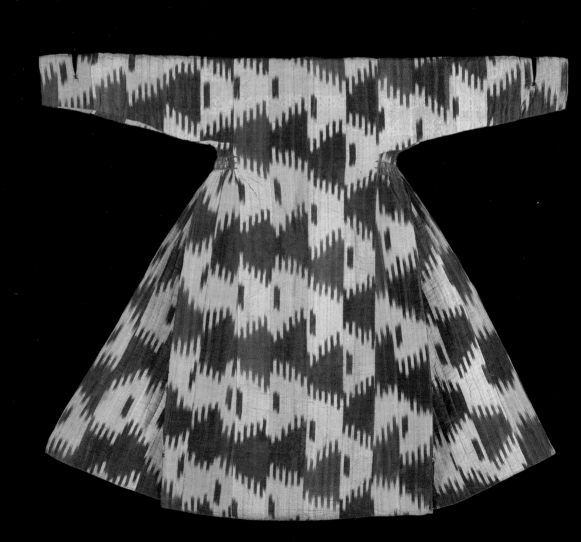

WOMAN'S ROBE

Second half 19th century
Central Asia, Uzbekistan, Fergana Valley
Inscription: Unidentified blue marks
Silk warp, cotton weft, polished,
Russian roller print cotton interior
82.2013

CAT. 5

WOMAN'S ROBE

Second half 19th century
Central Asia, Uzbekistan
Silk warp, cotton weft with egg wash glaze,
Russian roller print cotton interior
T.2014.569

CAT. 6

WINTER ROBE

19th century
Central Asia, Uzbekistan, Khwarezm
Silk warp, cotton weft with egg wash glaze,
Russian roller print cotton interior,
machine quilted
73.2013

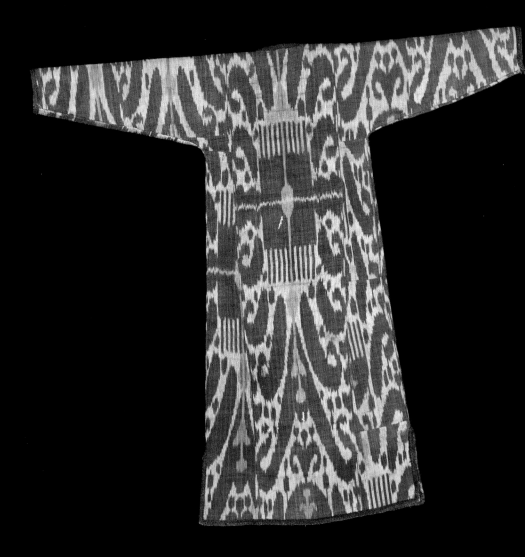

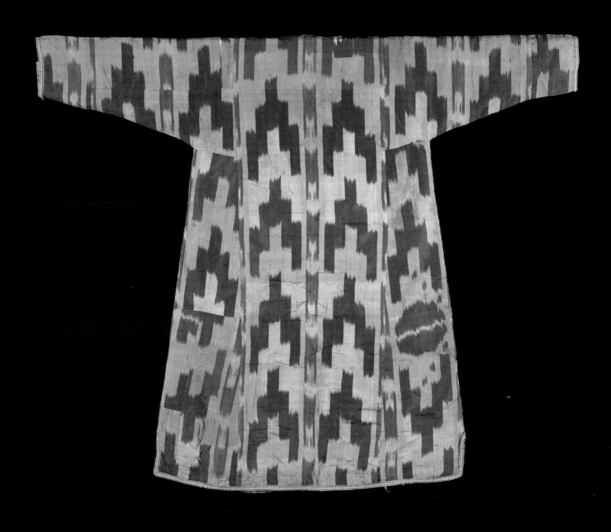

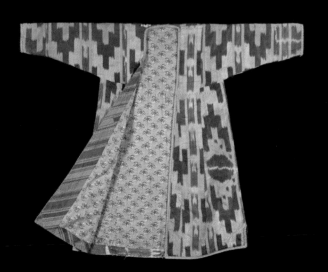

CAT. 7

ROBE

Late 19th century
Central Asia, Uzbekistan, Bukhara
Silk warp and weft *atlas* or *shahi* ikat,
Russian roller print cotton interior
72.2013

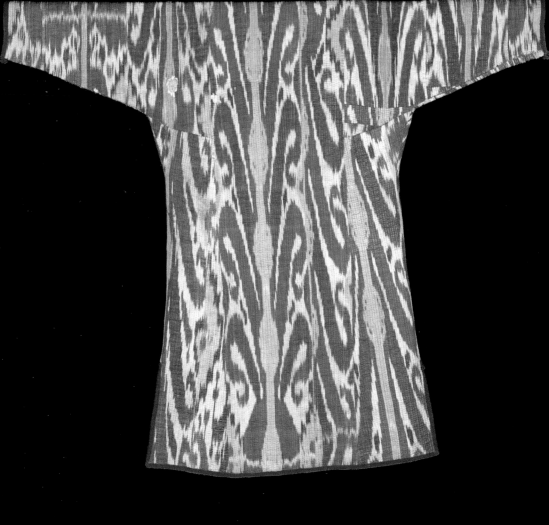

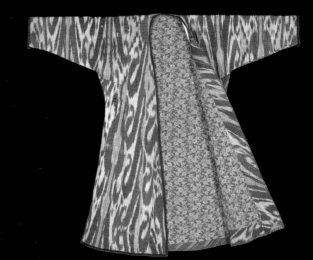

CAT. 8

ROBE

Second half 19th century
Central Asia, Uzbekistan, Khwarezm
Inscription: unidentified blue stamp
Silk warp, cotton weft,
Russian roller print cotton interior
81.2013

CAT. 9

WINTER ROBE

Late 19th century
Central Asia, Uzbekistan, Fergana Valley
Inscription on lining: Manufactured
by the Baranov Factory
Silk warp, cotton weft, Russian roller print
cotton interior, padded and machine quilted
80.2013

CAT. 10

ROBE

Late 19th–early 20th century
Central Asia, Uzbekistan,
Fergana Valley region
Silk warp and weft with egg wash glaze,
Russian roller print cotton interior
67.2013

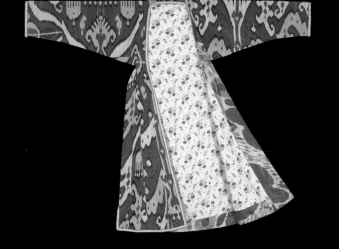

CAT. 11

WOMAN'S ROBE

Late 19th century
Central Asia, Uzbekistan, Bukhara
Silk warp and weft, Russian roller
print cotton interior
71.2013

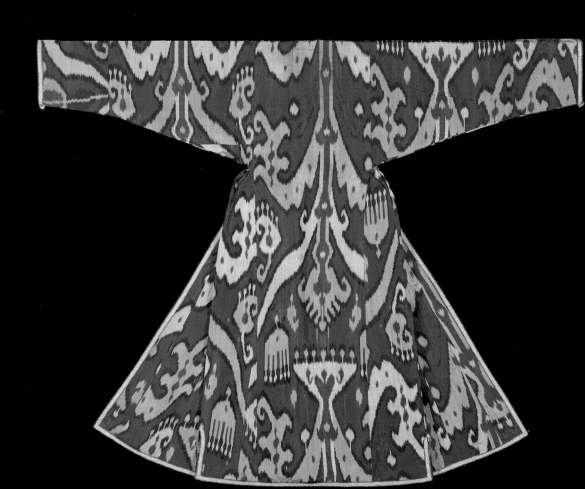

CAT. 12

WOMAN'S ROBE

Late 19th century
Central Asia, Uzbekistan, Bukhara
Silk warp, cotton weft with egg wash glaze,
Russian roller print cotton interior
75.2013

CAT. 13

ROBE

Second half 19th century
Central Asia, Uzbekistan, Bukhara
Silk warp, cotton weft *adras* ikat,
mixture of Russian printed cottons interior
77.2013

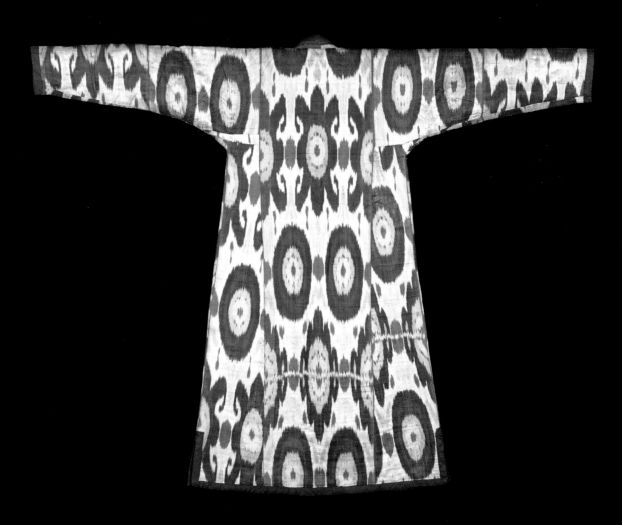

CAT. 14

ROBE

Second half 19th century
Central Asia, Uzbekistan, Bukhara
Silk warp, cotton weft, polished,
Russian roller print cotton interior
78.2013

CAT. 15

WINTER ROBE

Second half 19th century
Central Asia, Uzbekistan, Bukhara
Silk warp and weft,
Russian roller print cotton interior
T.2014.567

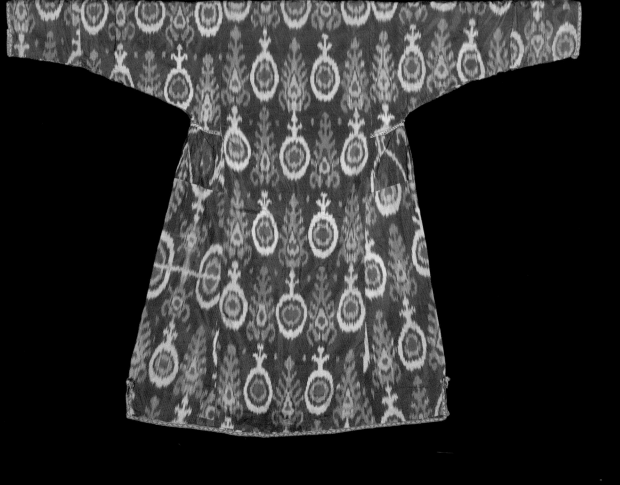

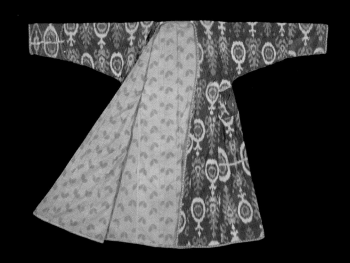

WOMAN'S ROBE

Second half 19th century
Central Asia, Uzbekistan
Silk warp and weft,
Russian roller print cotton interior
T.2014.568

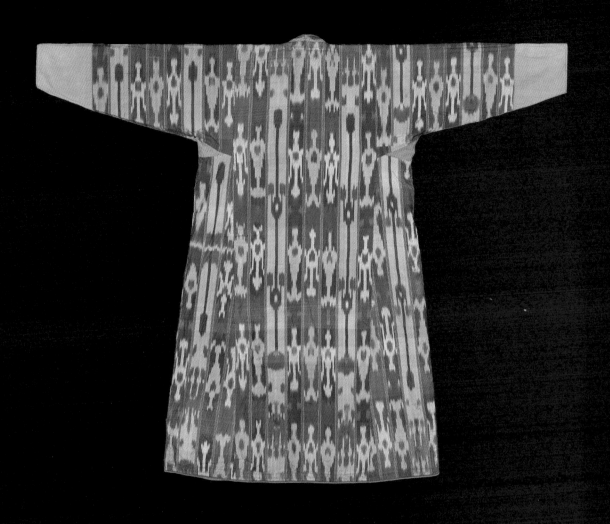

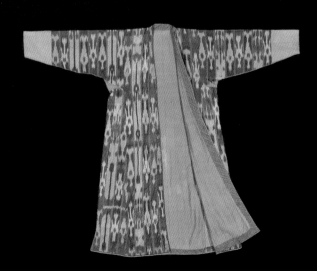

CAT. 17

ROBE

Late 19th century
Central Asia, Uzbekistan
Silk warp, cotton weft *atlas* ikat,
cotton interior
84.2013

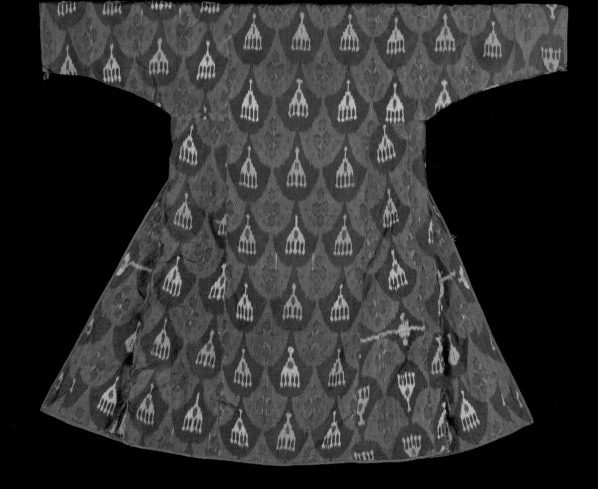

WOMAN'S ROBE

Late 19th century
Central Asia, Uzbekistan
Silk warp and weft, polished,
Russian roller print cotton interior
74.2013

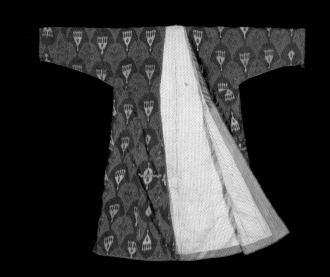

CAT. 20

WOMAN'S ROBE

Second half 19th century
Central Asia, Uzbekistan, Bukhara
Silk warp and weft, polished,
Russian roller print cotton interior
85.2013

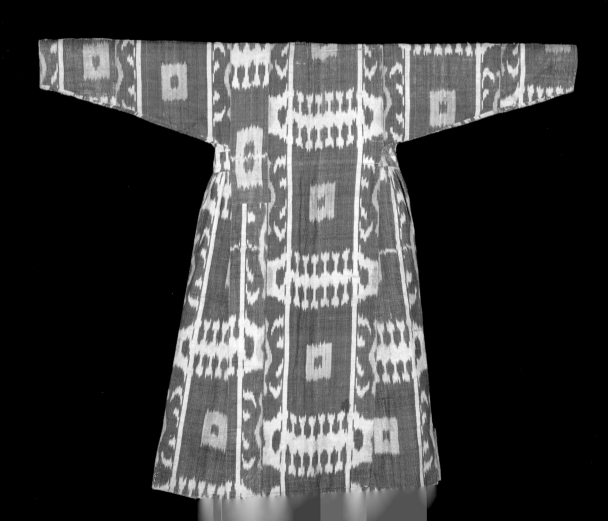

CAT. 21

ROBE

Late 19th century
Central Asia, Uzbekistan, Bukhara
Silk warp and indigo-dyed
cotton weft *adras* ikat,
Russian roller print cotton interior
1031.2013

CAT. 22

WOMAN'S ROBE

Second half 19th century
Central Asia, Uzbekistan, Bukhara
Silk warp and weft *atlas* ikat,
Russian roller print cotton interior
1032.2013

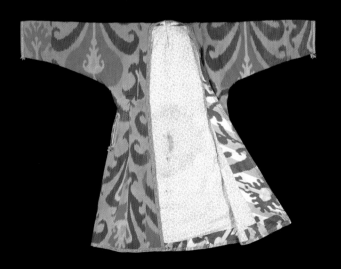

CAT. 23

WOMAN'S ROBE

Second half 19th century
Central Asia, Uzbekistan, Bukhara
Silk warp and weft *atlas* ikat,
Russian roller print cotton interior
1033.2013

CAT. 24

ROBE

Late 19th century
Central Asia, Uzbekistan,
Fergana Valley or Samarkand
Silk warp and weft,
Russian roller print cotton interior
70.2013

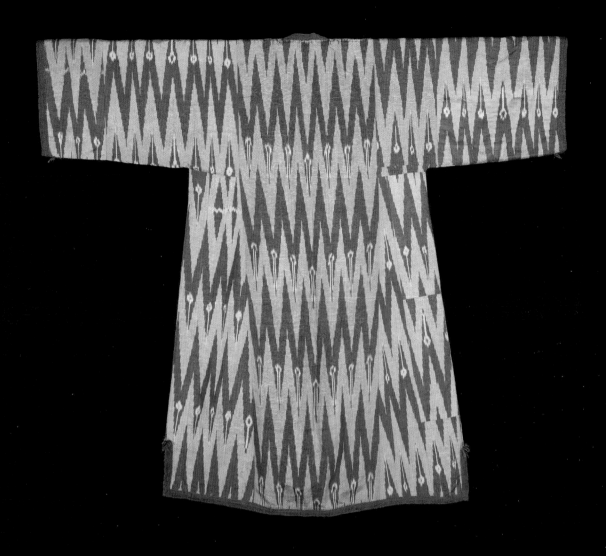

CAT. 25

WOMAN'S ROBE

Second half 19th century
Central Asia, Uzbekistan
Silk warp, cotton weft, Russian roller print
cotton interior, cotton edging and fringe
T.2015.218

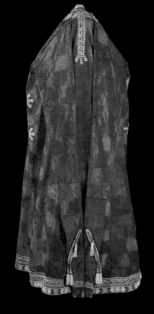

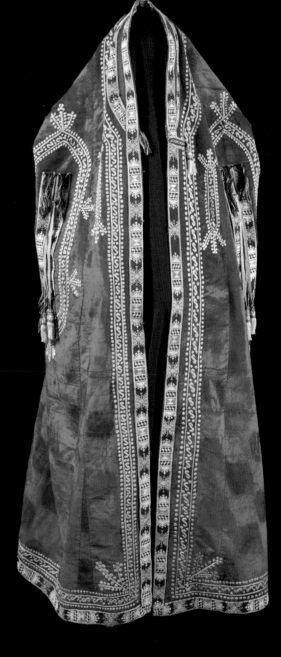

CAT. 26

PARANJA or FARANJI

Late 19th–early 20th century
Central Asia, Uzbekistan, Samarkand (?)
Silk warp and weft, silk velvet
with wool and cotton velvets
86.2013

CAT. 27

WALL HANGING

Second half 19th century
Central Asia, Uzbekistan
Velvet ikat
T.2015.232

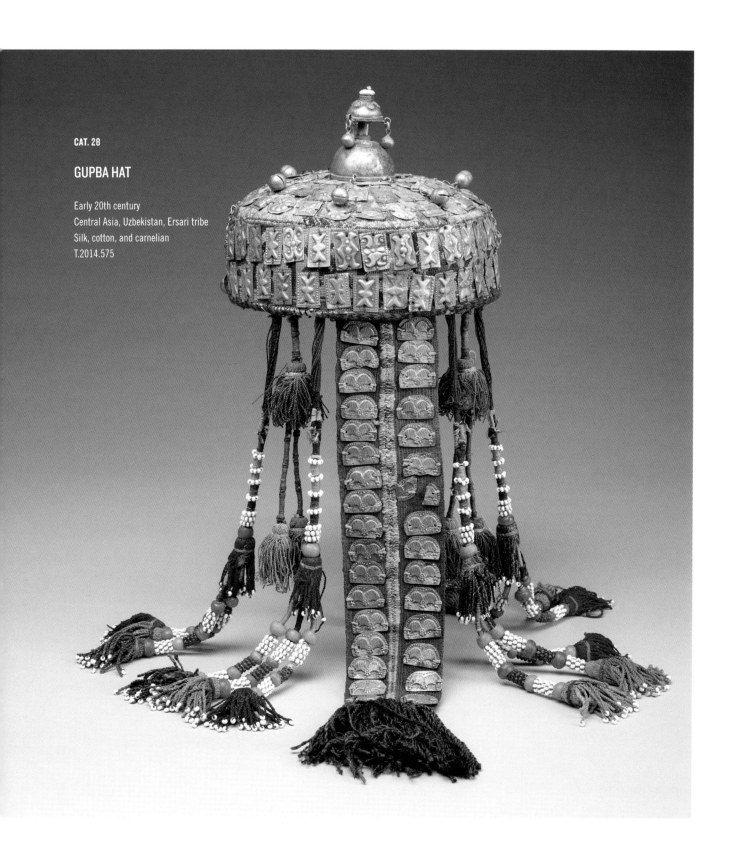

CAT. 28

GUPBA HAT

Early 20th century
Central Asia, Uzbekistan, Ersari tribe
Silk, cotton, and carnelian
T.2014.575

66 —

CAT. 29

GUPBA HAT

Early 20th century
Central Asia, Uzbekistan or Turkmenistan
Silk, cotton, and carnelian
88.2013

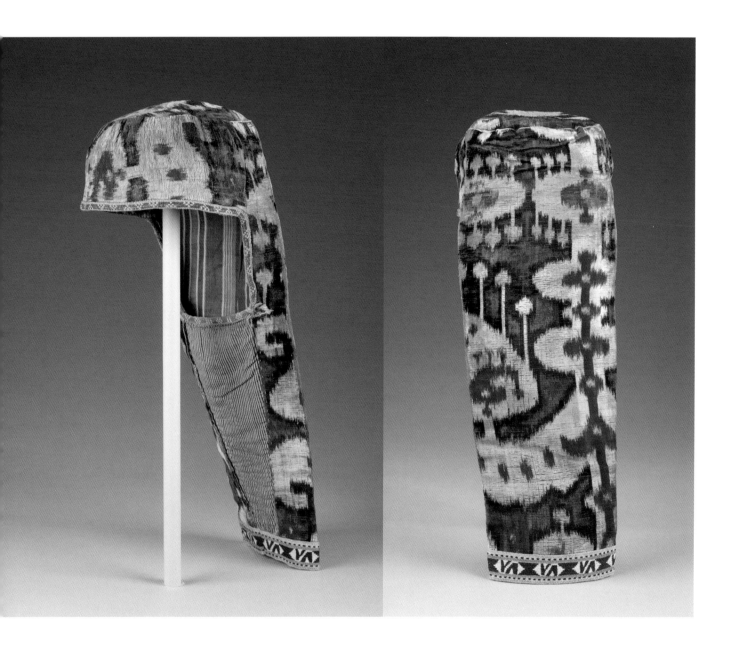

CAT. 30

BRIDAL HAT

Late 19th century
Central Asia, Uzbekistan
Silk velvet, Bakhmal
68.2013

BRIDAL HAT

Late 19th century
Central Asia, Uzbekistan, Bukhara
Dyed velvet, metallic thread, and knitted ribbon
1035.2013

CAT. 32

HAT

Early 20th century
Central Asia, Uzbekistan
Dyed velvet, metallic thread, and knitted ribbon
1036.2013

CAT. 33

BRIDAL HAT

Late 19th century
Central Asia, Uzbekistan
Silk and metallic thread
1037.2013

CAT. 34

VEIL

Early 20th century
Central Asia, Uzbekistan
Cotton, glass, and metal
87.2013

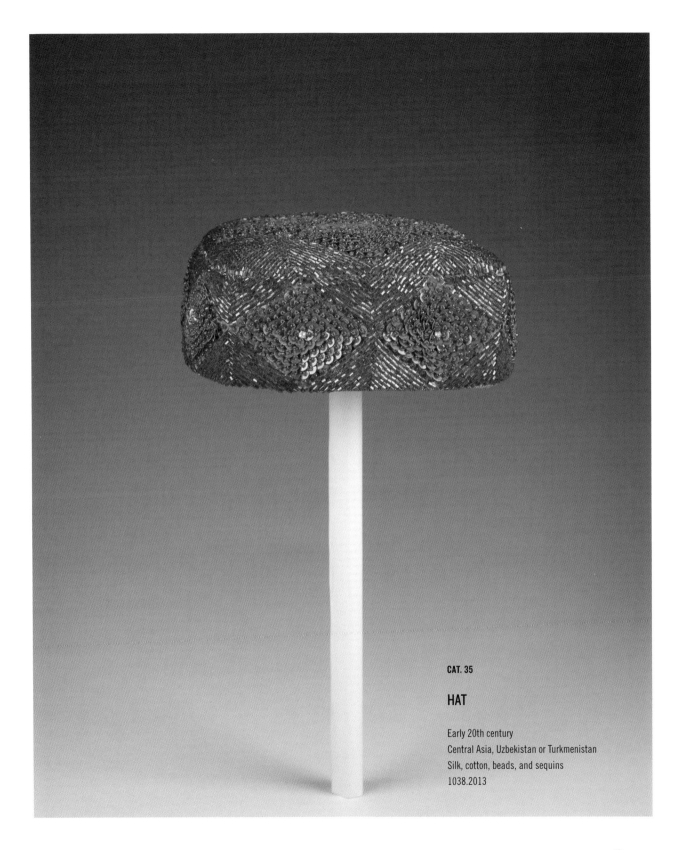

CAT. 35

HAT

Early 20th century
Central Asia, Uzbekistan or Turkmenistan
Silk, cotton, beads, and sequins
1038.2013

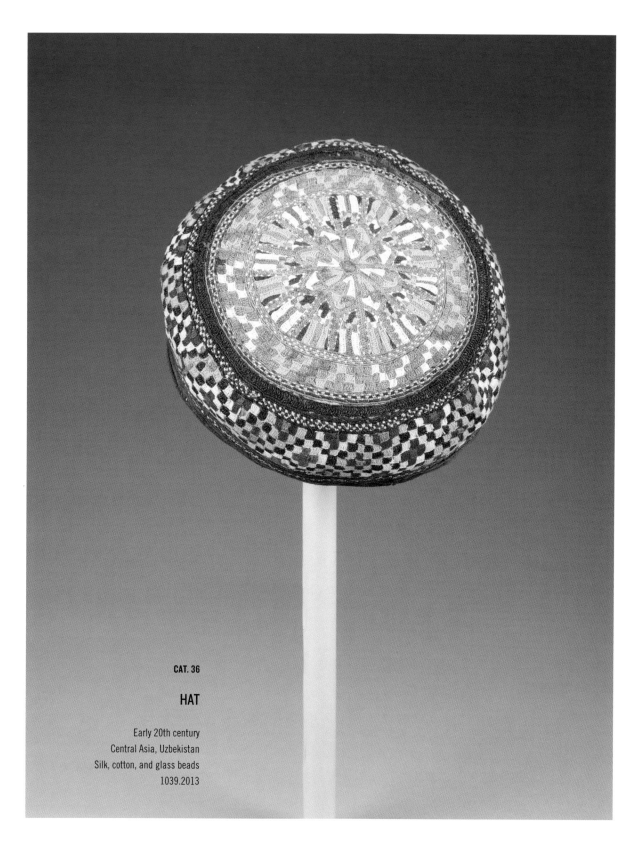

CAT. 36

HAT

Early 20th century
Central Asia, Uzbekistan
Silk, cotton, and glass beads
1039.2013

CAT. 37

HAT

Early 20th century
Central Asia, Uzbekistan, Lakai tribe (?)
Cotton and glass beads
1040.2013

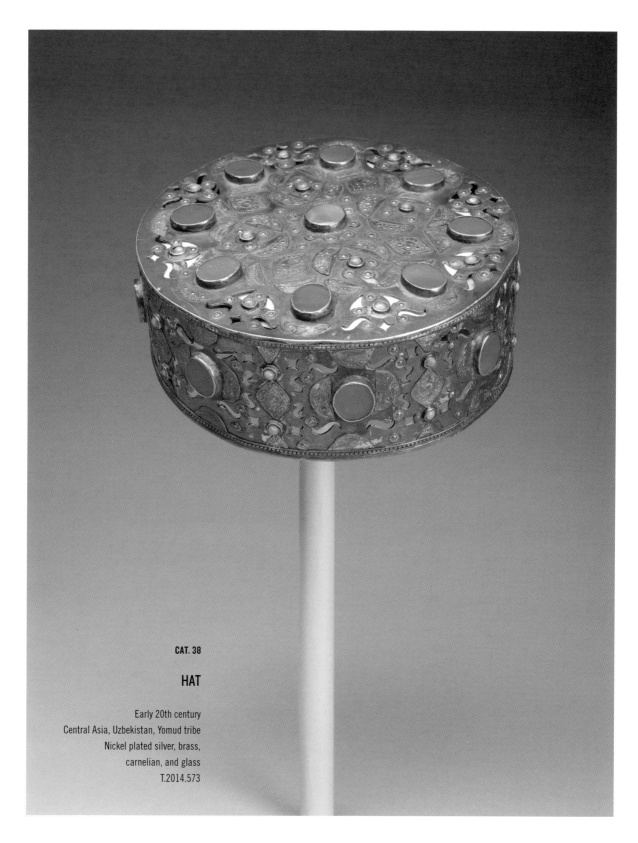

CAT. 38

HAT

Early 20th century
Central Asia, Uzbekistan, Yomud tribe
Nickel plated silver, brass,
carnelian, and glass
T.2014.573

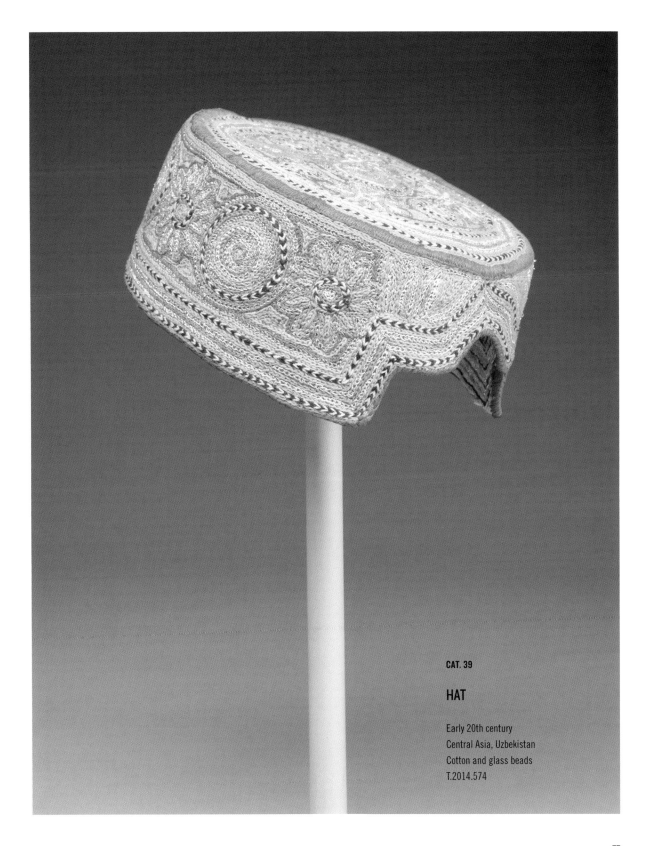

CAT. 39

HAT

Early 20th century
Central Asia, Uzbekistan
Cotton and glass beads
T.2014.574

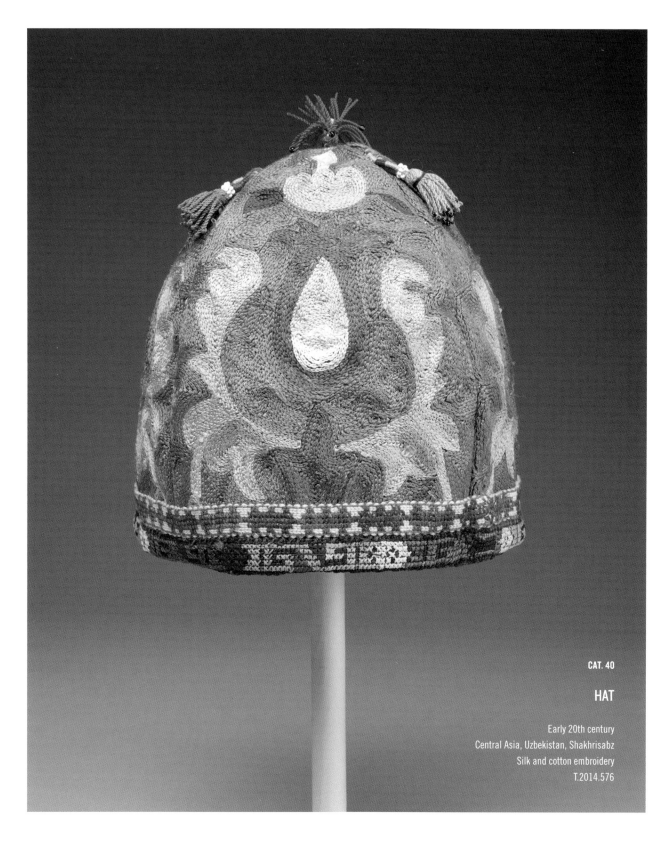

CAT. 40

HAT

Early 20th century
Central Asia, Uzbekistan, Shakhrisabz
Silk and cotton embroidery
T.2014.576

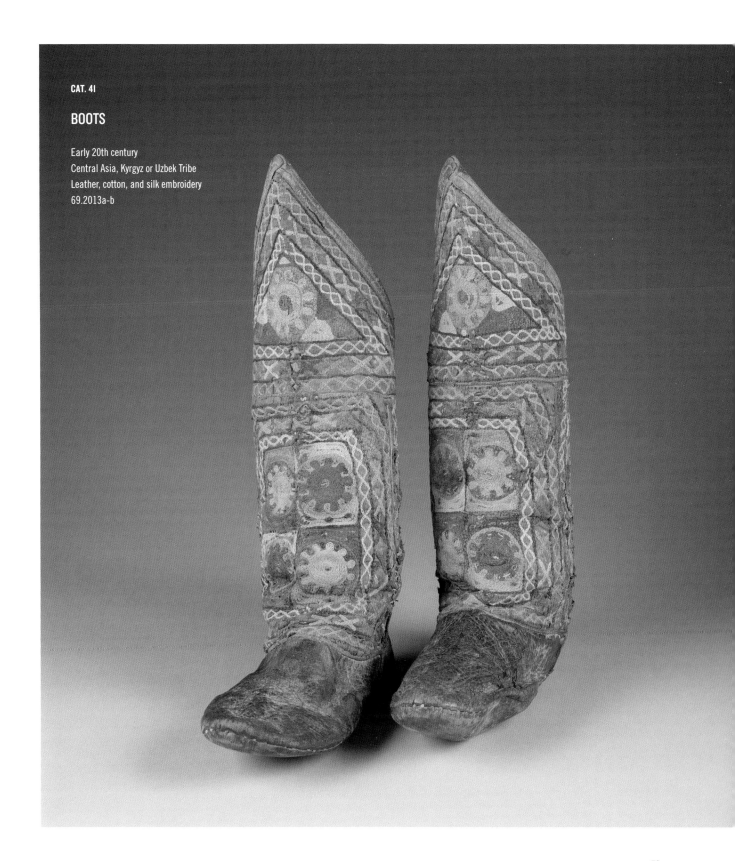

CAT. 41

BOOTS

Early 20th century
Central Asia, Kyrgyz or Uzbek Tribe
Leather, cotton, and silk embroidery
69.2013a-b

CAT. 42

BOOTS

Late 19th century
Central Asia, Uzbekistan, Bukhara
Leather, cotton, and silver embroidery
1034.2013a-b

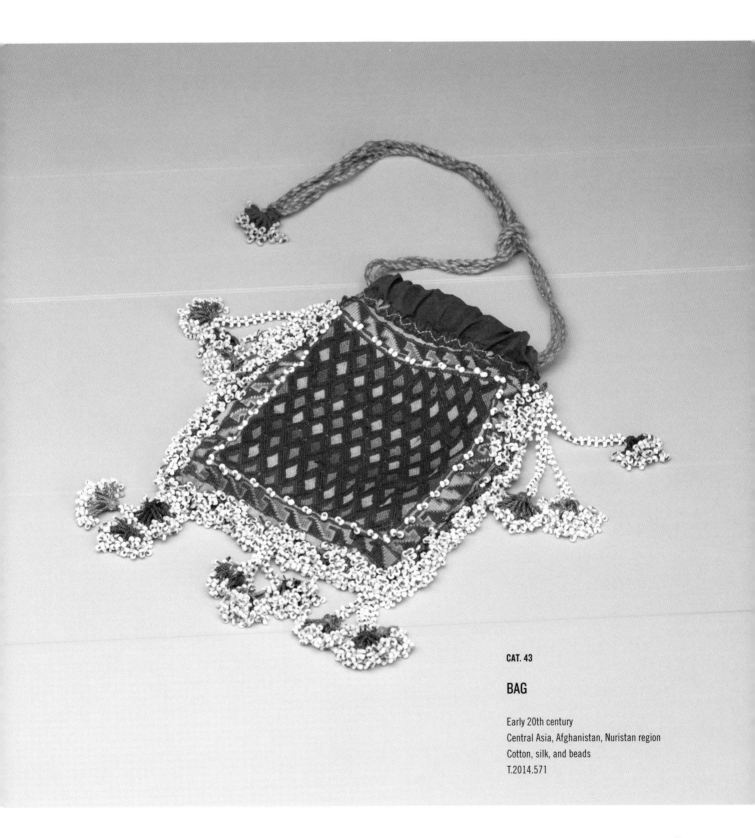

CAT. 43

BAG

Early 20th century
Central Asia, Afghanistan, Nuristan region
Cotton, silk, and beads
T.2014.571

BAG

Late 19th century
Central Asia, Uzbekistan, Lakai tribe
Cotton, silk, and beads
T.2014.572

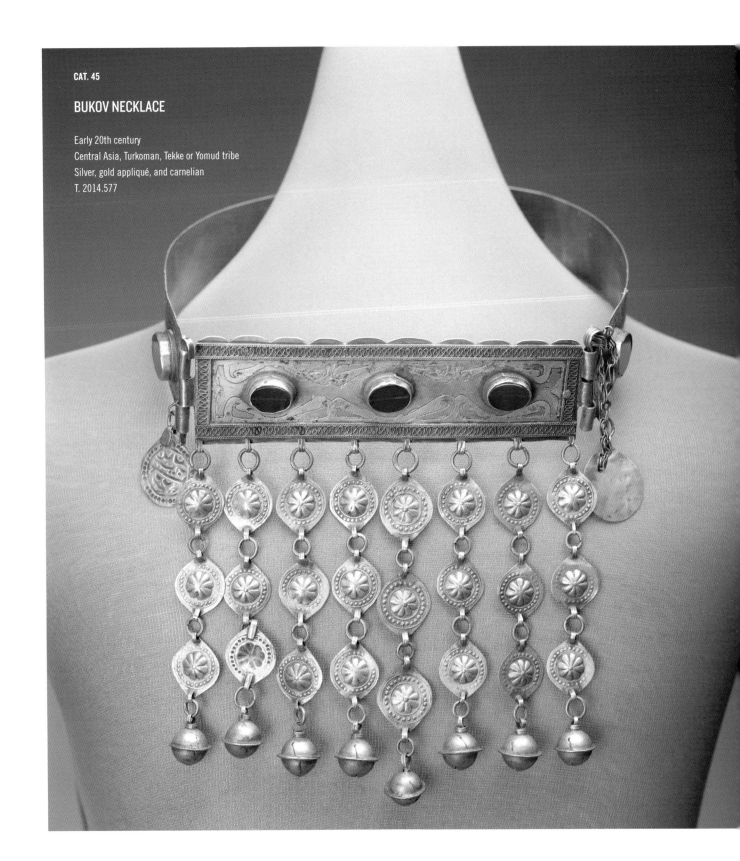

BUKOV NECKLACE

Early 20th century
Central Asia, Turkoman, Tekke or Yomud tribe
Silver, gold appliqué, and carnelian
T. 2014.577

CAT. 46

ADAMLYK PENDANT

Late 19th century
Central Asia, Turkoman
Silver, gold appliqué, and carnelian
T.2014.578

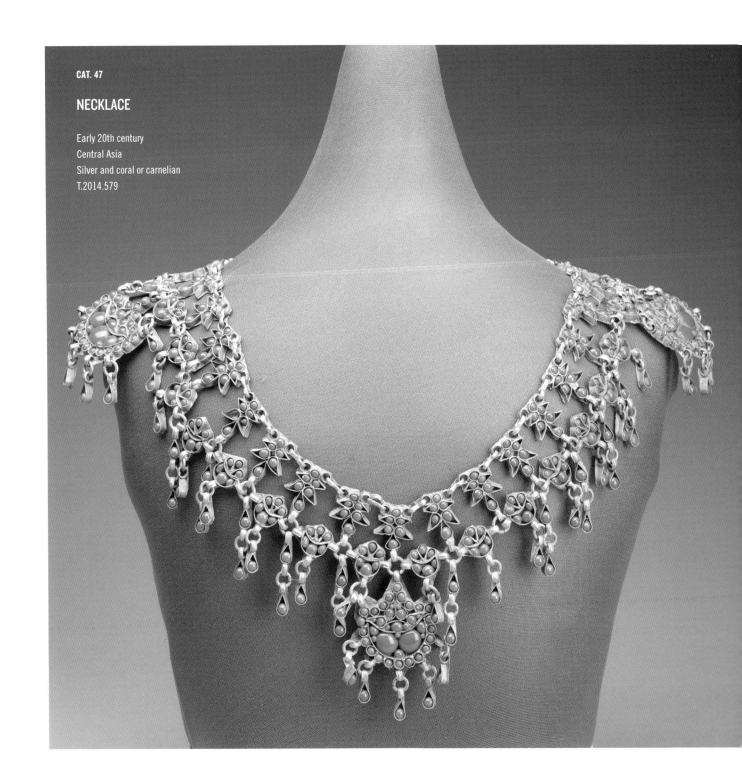

NECKLACE

Early 20th century
Central Asia
Silver and coral or carnelian
T.2014.579

CAT. 48

PENDANT

Early 20th century
Central Asia
Silver and carnelian
T.2014.580

CAT. 49

NECKLACE

Early 20th century
Central Asia, Uzbekistan,
Bukhara (?)
Silver, turquoise,
carnelian, and enamel
T.2014.581

CAT. 50

PENDANT

Early 20th century
Central Asia, Turkoman or Tekke Tribe
Silver, gold appliqué, and carnelian
T.2014.582

BRACELET

Early 20th century
Central Asia, Uzbekistan, Karakalpak tribe (?)
Silver, turquoise, and carnelian
T.2014.583

CAT. 52

MOSKA EARRINGS

Early 20th century
Central Asia
Silver and coral
T. 2014.584a&b

CAT. 53

NECKLACE

Early 20th century
Central Asia
Silver
T.2014.585

CAT. 55

NECKLACE

Early 20th century
Central Asia
Silver, gold appliqué,
and carnelian
T.2015.228

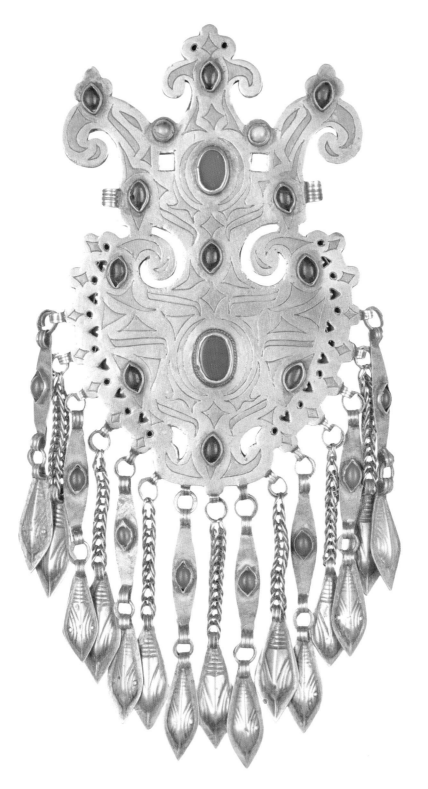

CAT. 56

PENDANT

Early 20th century
Central Asia
Silver, gold appliqué,
carnelian, and glass
T.2015.230

CAT. 57

BUTTON

Early 20th century
Central Asia
Silver, gold appliqué,
and glass
T.2015.231

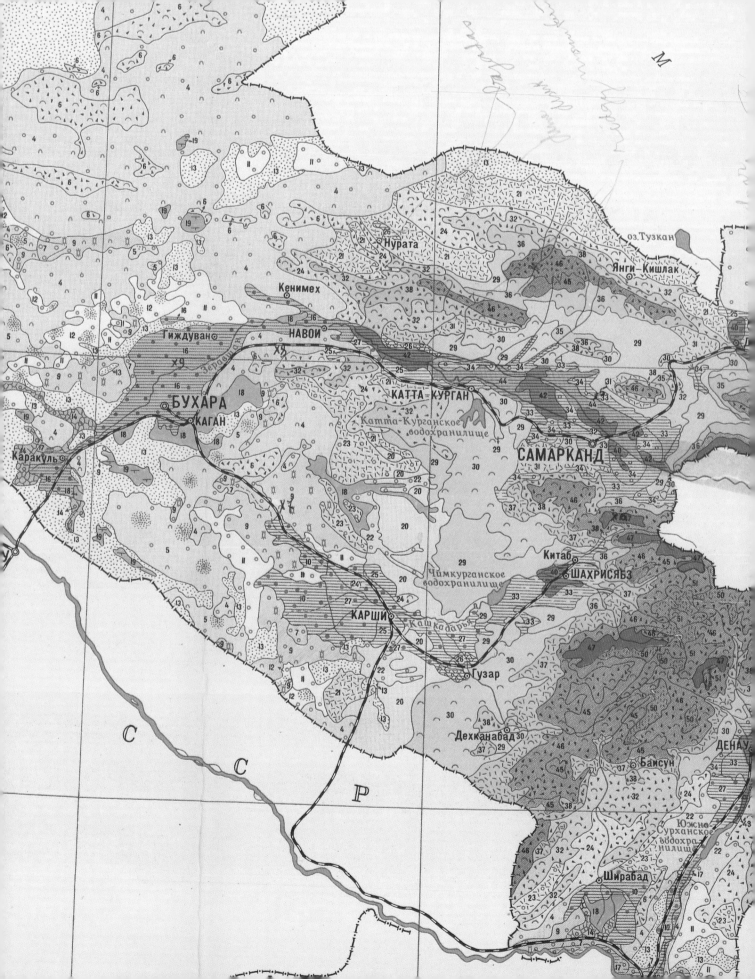